Easy Craft Ideas for Kids

26 Fun-Filled Arts and Crafts Projects for Kids of All Ages

by Wendy Livestone

Table of Contents

Introduction 1

Chapter 1: Paper Kite 7

Chapter 2: Pet Rock 11

Chapter 3: Live Plant Terrarium 15

Chapter 4: Kool Aid Pasta 19

Chapter 5: Pasta Jewelry/Candy Jewelry 23

Chapter 6: Melted Crayon Art 27

Chapter 7: Crayon Transfers 31

Chapter 8: Dreamcatchers 35

Chapter 9: Maracas 39

Chapter 10: Tin Lanterns 43

Chapter 11: Acorn Jewels 47

Chapter 12: Glitter Jars 51

Chapter 13: No Plug Lava Lamp 55

Chapter 14: Rainbow Milk 59

Chapter 15: Fizzy Volcano 63

Chapter 16: Crayon Etching Art 67

Chapter 17: Glittery Play Dough 71

Chapter 18: Duct Tape Magnets 75

Chapter 19: Monster Claws 79

Chapter 20: Snow Globes 83

Chapter 21: Paper Bouquets 87

Chapter 22: Papier Mâché 91

Chapter 23: Countdown Paper Chains 95

Chapter 24: Friendship Bracelets 97

Chapter 25: Tie Dye T-shirts 101

Chapter 26: Water Xylophone 103

Conclusion 105

Introduction

The collection of crafts in this book is suitable for children of all ages. Although younger kids are the primary target group, the collection is also good for older children or even teenagers, as most of the projects are simple enough for older children to act as supervisors for the younger ones. In addition, there are a few crafts listed in here that the older kids, even teenagers, will surely enjoy, such as the kite, terrarium, and tie dye T-shirts. Besides, who knows? Being in a supervisory position could also bring back nostalgic memories for the older children who are helpers.

Most of the projects in this book are geared towards creating "useful" items, as much as possible. When I was a child, I found it much more enjoyable making something that could be used later on. With any craft listed here, I would advise encouraging the child to be as creative as possible in his or her expression. Feel free to embellish and add even more sparkle or decoration. Don't just stop at glitter and paper; add googly eyes, glue-able gems, pipe cleaners…anything you can think of to get the imagination going.

As for the more artistic crafts, such as the crayon etching or crayon transfers, give the children prompts that encourage them to think creatively. For example, have them look around the room, observe what they see, and draw it. Or make a self portrait, or draw something or someone that is important to them.

And remember, these activities are just a starting point. It's only natural that you'll think of a fun riff on these projects, or if one activity triggers an idea for an entirely new one, go for it! The possibilities are endless.

© Copyright 2015 by Miafn LLC - All rights reserved.

This document is geared towards providing reliable information in regards to the topic and issue covered. The publication is sold with the idea that the publisher is not required to render accounting, officially permitted, or otherwise, qualified services. If advice is necessary, legal or professional, a practiced individual in the profession should be ordered.

- From a Declaration of Principles which was accepted and approved equally by a Committee of the American Bar Association and a Committee of Publishers and Associations.

In no way is it legal to reproduce, duplicate, or transmit any part of this document in either electronic means or in printed format. Recording of this publication is strictly prohibited and any storage of this document is not allowed unless with written permission from the publisher. All rights reserved.

The information provided herein is stated to be truthful and consistent, in that any liability, in terms of inattention or otherwise, by any usage or abuse of any policies, processes, or directions contained within is solely and completely the responsibility of the recipient reader. Under no circumstances will any legal responsibility or blame be held against the publisher for any reparation, damages, or monetary loss due to the information herein, either directly or indirectly.

Respective authors own all copyrights not held by the publisher.

The information herein is offered for informational purposes solely, and is universal as so. The presentation of the information is without contract or any type of guarantee assurance.

The trademarks that are used are without any consent, and the publication of the trademark is without permission or backing by the trademark owner. All trademarks and brands within this book are for clarifying purposes only and are the owned by the owners themselves, not affiliated with this document.

Chapter 1: Paper Kite

This is a craft for older kids, or for younger kids with appropriate supervision.

You will need:

- A standard 8.5x11 piece of computer paper, preferably in a fun color. Card stock (thicker paper) is going to hold up a bit better. Encourage the child to draw fun designs on it if they like.

- A wooden skewer or plastic drinking straw

- Kite string or fishing line

- Wide ribbon or surveyors tape

- Scissors

- Hole punch

- Tape (again, in a fun color)

Fold the piece of paper in half, hamburger style. Mark a point on the top, one inch from the fold, and on the bottom at about the same spot, but at a diagonal. Draw a diagonal line to connect the two dots, and help your child imagine it. Fold the top corner down along the line. Flip the paper and fold the other side in the same way. Flip the paper back over to its original side and tape it along the seam to hold the fold in place. Lay the skewer across the top of the kite, which should be evident by now, and tape it into place. If the skewer sticks out too much, help your child trim it to size. Flip the kite back over, straighten it out, and pick a spot a third of the way down the spine, which you will mark with a pen. This is where you're going to punch a hole to run the kite string. Put tape around each side to reinforce it after you punch the hole, and then run the string. Help your child tie a really strong knot. Then tape your kite tail to the end of the kite. Play around with the length. The sturdier the tail, the shorter it will need to be. You'll have to observe the wind conditions before you can truly determine the length you will need.

Chapter 2: Pet Rock

You will need:

- Rocks (make sure they are a good size, and mostly flat)

- Washable paint (I find that tempera works best)

- Paper

- Googly eyes

- Pompoms

- Glitter

- Glue-on gemstones

- Glue (tacky glue or Elmer's school glue, nothing toxic)

- Pipe cleaners

- Any other fun craft store finds

This craft is really a no brainer, it's up to the child to glue whatever they want wherever they want on their rocks. First things first, you'll want to have the child wash the rocks to get all the dirt off. Second is the painting part. Make sure you lay the rock down on plenty of paper to prevent making a mess. If the child gets super creative, they may even want to keep their paper as its own masterpiece. After the paint is dry, let them have free rein with all the decorations at their disposal. Remember, the rock doesn't just have to have two eyes or two antennae. Let them do as they please, but you may still want to help them out with glue application to avoid huge messes. After they're done, make sure they let the pet rock dry completely before playing with it. Ask them where their rock lives, what it does for fun, what its friends look like, etc.

Chapter 3: Live Plant Terrarium

This is another activity that may be more fun for older kids, but if you do choose to involve smaller children, it may be wise to omit the cactus from the mix. Otherwise, this can really be a fun and easy way to teach young kids about how to take care of living things. Plus, succulents and cacti are easy to take care of. If a child does well with this, they can probably move on to a small garden, with plants such as carrots and tomatoes.

You will need:

- A clear glass jar (Cool shapes are fun)

- Pebbles

- Succulent plants (and cacti if you're working with older kids)

- Succulent potting soil

- Colored sand

- Spoon

Fill up the bottom of your jar with about an inch and a half of pebbles. Add about two and a half inches of potting soil. Take hold of your first plant and brush off whatever excess dust or soil that might be clinging to it. Using the spoon, make a hole large enough for the plant, and plan for it to have about an inch of room on either side to grow. It's typically best to start with your largest plant and add smaller plants around it. After you've placed each plant in the hole you've made, tamp the surrounding soil down to hold it firmly down. Have fun with the way you arrange it. If you do choose to include cacti with small kids involved, you could always plant it for them but just ask them where they would like it placed. After you're finished, add a quarter inch of sand on top.

All the children will need to do for upkeep is to put it in direct sunlight and water it every two weeks or when the soil is dry to the touch. Easy!

Chapter 4: Kool Aid Pasta

The activity in this chapter is going to be necessary for the activity in the following chapter. In order to make pasta jewelry, you're going to need pasta. When I was a child, teachers often left the pasta in its original color and integrated some tricolor pasta, as well as water soluble paints for us to use. While some kids may like the plain or tricolor pasta, a new option for making it more fun is to dye it with Kool Aid, which does require some adult (or at least teenage) supervision. After you've had the children help with dyeing the pasta and it has dried completely, I would still suggest allowing them to paint and/or glitter up the pasta before making jewelry out of it.

What you will need is:

- Dry pasta (for younger kids, I would suggest something large and easier to string, like penne. Older kids, five and up, might be able to handle smaller pastas like elbow pasta. If you're unsure, get a variety).

- Kool Aid packets of your color choice

- 1 tablespoon of rubbing alcohol

- Gallon Ziplock bags

- Tin foil

- Baking sheet

Put the pasta in the Ziplock bag and add one color of Kool Aid. If you plan on doing multiple colors you should have multiple bags of pasta. Let the kids do this first part, then you add the tablespoon of rubbing alcohol. You will need a tablespoon per bag. This is going to help the color adhere to the pasta. Close the bag and have the child shake it up. You want to let the pasta sit in the bag for at least ten minutes so it takes in the color.

In the meantime, set up your baking sheet with tin foil to hold your pasta, and after it's nice and dyed, you're going to set it on the baking sheet for a few hours to dry. After about six hours, it should be good to go, and you can give it to the child to decorate further or to make macaroni jewelry from.

Chapter 5: Pasta Jewelry/Candy Jewelry

All you need for this activity is the dyed pasta from the previous chapter. Or alternatively, if you would like to make candy jewelry, you'll need things like:

- Peach rings
- Twizzlers
- Any candy that has a hole in it
- Jelly beans
- Smarties or sweet tarts
- Stretchy string or thicker yarn for pasta bracelets
- A small needle for jelly beans and/or smarties

Measure out some lengths of string or yarn, depending on materials and/or preference, using the child's arm as a reference. Knot the string well so that your materials will not fall off, and give the child a piece of string. Let them pick from the variety of materials to create their jewelry.

If they want to make use of the jelly beans and/or smarties, adult supervision will be required to poke holes in the candy. Using a small needle, poke holes in the candy; wipe the needle off after every few pieces so that it doesn't gunk up. The children will then be able to string it on the thinner stretchy string easily. Watch them as they work, and when they've only got about half an inch of string left, help knot their jewelry off.

A variation is using pipe cleaners instead of yarn, you could also include pony beads instead.

Chapter 6: Melted Crayon Art

This project will require adult supervision due to the hot glue gun involved, but otherwise it is very simple.

You will need:

- Hot glue gun

- Blow dryer

- Stretched canvas

- Crayons (I would suggest a 24 pack or more for the kids to choose from)

Typically the crayons are arranged right at the top of the canvas, but you should encourage the kids to pick out whatever colors they want and arrange them wherever they want on the canvas. Just explain to them that when they are done, the crayons are going to drip down the canvas and create original art.

After they have made their arrangements, go around and help the kids glue down their crayons. An easy way to have them help do this is to put the glob of glue down and allow them to very carefully stick the crayon down on top of it. In order to get the most effective drip, have the kids place the crayons tip down.

Now comes the fun part. In order to create the art, you'll want to have the kids turn on a blow dryer on high and point it downwards onto the crayons. This can be a great exercise of having patience, as it can take several minutes for the crayons to begin to soften and melt. When they do, tell the kids to pay attention to how the direction and closeness of the heat makes the direction of the crayon spatter change. Have them adjust it as they want, until they are satisfied with how it looks.

To finish, all you have to do is allow it to dry completely.

Chapter 7: Crayon Transfers

This is kind of similar to an art exercise I used to really enjoy as a little kid, which I think this is kind of a riff on. It's a really simple way, like the above craft, to make use of crayons to create some pretty cool and unique art that will wow your kids.

You will need:

- Crayons
- White paper
- A pencil or ballpoint pen

Let your child create whatever patterns they would like on a sheet of paper. It can literally be anything they want, but make sure that you instruct them to press down very, very hard. The more wax they can get down onto the paper, the better. Brush off any extra bits of crayon there may be on the paper, and then flip your colored paper over onto a sheet of clean white paper. Using the pen or pencil, have your child press down hard as they draw whatever it is they want to. The color will transfer onto the fresh paper, showing off the new drawing.

You could then hang them on the refrigerator or cut the shapes out to create garlands or jewelry.

Chapter 8: Dreamcatchers

Dreamcatchers are super cute and kids love them. They're incredibly simple to make and can be made into any shape, they just require a little bit of adult supervision since they require the use of wire.

You will need:

- Paper covered wire

- Yarn

- Scissors

- Beads and feathers, which are optional, but add a nice touch

Help the children cut the wire into various sizes and bend it into various shapes. Circles, ovals, hearts, or even stars are good ideas. After the wire is bent into shape, wrap the first layer of yarn around the frame, knotting it securely. Continue wrapping different colored yarn around the frame until you or your child is satisfied. When finished, leave about a foot or so of yarn at the top and tie off a knot so that it can be hung. You could even create an entire mobile of dreamcatchers. If your child would like to add feathers or beads, all you have to do is add some lengths of string to the bottom of the dreamcatcher and allow them to string on whatever they want, knotting each string securely. Then, hang it up and you're done.

Chapter 9: Maracas

This is a multipurpose craft, especially for very creative or musically inclined children. These maracas are easy and mess-free to make, and can be made at any time of year although it may be especially good to do so around Easter, because it uses plastic Easter eggs.

You will need:

- Plastic eggs

- Plastic spoons

- Washi tape/ duck tape/ any other fun colored or patterned tape

- Rice/dry beans or any other dry rattling object

This project is relatively simple: the kids will fill up one half of each plastic egg with rice, beans, or whatever is available. Make sure you leave enough space in the egg to still be able to seal it back up.

Then take two plastic spoons and sandwich the egg between it. You might have to help the child with this part, as you begin taping the spoons to the egg. You just need enough to secure it in place. Then, wrap it around the top, following the shape of the egg to make the shape of the maraca more evident. Keep going until it's nice and thick and you've also covered the top of the handle. Simple!

Chapter 10: Tin Lanterns

Tin lanterns are super cute, and they always remind me of early summer nights or of the memorial tea lights used at Relay For Life. This is a great project for teenagers and parents, as nailing is involved. Depending on the age of the child, you could either use real tea lights or battery-powered ones. The great thing about this project is that it's appropriate for all ages, even adults.

You will need:

- A tin can

- A hammer

- Nails

- Markers

- A towel

- Tea lights (either battery-powered or candles)

- Wire

One trick I've learned is to fill up the cans with water and stick them in the freezer for a few hours. It will help prevent the can from denting when you design it later. Take your can out of the freezer and have your child draw their design onto the can using the marker. You place the nail over a portion of the design and begin to very carefully hammer, moving along the design as you go. With smaller children or children with low dexterity, you might want to have them hold onto the nail as you tap gently with the hammer.

Once you finish the design, dump out the ice, and add your tea light and wire handle (if you want). If you've chosen to use an actual tea light instead of battery-powered ones, now may be an optimal time to teach older children how to safely light a candle and place it in the lantern. If you do choose real candles, make sure that if they're placed outside, somewhere where they won't blow over. If you make a few, they'll create quite a lovely atmosphere, and with the handles, you could even hang them from porch railings or tree branches.

Chapter 11: Acorn Jewels

This is an awesome new project that, like the Kool Aid pasta, can be used to make all sorts of awesome jewelry. All you'd have to do is drill a little hole in the top allow you to string it.

You will need:

- Acorn caps

- Glue

- Markers

- Rice

To start off, this is a great project to go outside for, especially in fall. Go with your children to look for acorn caps to work with. Get some really pigmented markers, maybe even some metallics to add to that jewel-like quality. Have the children color in the acorn cap. (Not the outside, but the curved underside, although they of course can color the top too). After the acorns are fully colored, have the children place them into the rice to hold them up, and fill up the cap with the school glue. The marker pigment will seep in to color the glue. Let the acorns sit in the rice until the glue has completely dried.

After they're dry, they're good for all kinds of activities your child may want them for, but I still maintain that they'd be really pretty as pendants for jewelry. Ask your child if they also want to add glitter on the jewels.

Chapter 12: Glitter Jars

This is one of those projects that really has no practical use, but is good for children because the glitter is enticing and distracting, and opening bottles is good for training the fine motor skills of small kids. This actually reminds me of a jar version of those little plastic squishy toys we used to all obsess over in the 90s.

You will need:

- A mason jar
- Glitter glue
- Glitter
- Warm water
- Plastic toys (optional)

Feel free to use multiple colors of glitter glue and loose glitter. Start out by putting the glitter glue into the jar, then add in the hot water. You really want it to be almost boiling, so that the glitter glue doesn't clump up but make sure you put the water in a cup that's going to be easy for a child to pour from and that they can't burn themselves on. A coffee thermos may be optimal. After they've added the water and stirred in the glitter glue a bit, let them add the loose glitter. Then, they can also add heat resistant plastic toys. If you don't mind your child getting a little bit messy, then you can allow them to put their hands into the jar to play with the toys as a soothing exercise when the water has cooled down a bit. When they're finished, put the cap on the jar. They can now shake it and swirl it whenever they want.

Chapter 13: No Plug Lava Lamp

This project is somewhat similar to the above one, but with different ingredients, and the oil creates the swirling effect of a real lava lamp.

You will need:

- Mason jars
- Water
- Vegetable oil
- Food coloring
- Alka Seltzer tablets
- Spoon

Fill up the Mason jar a third of the way with water, then add food coloring. Allow your child to fill up the jar almost the rest of the way with oil. They will enjoy the way that the two substances resist each other.

Then have the child break up the Alka Seltzer tablet and drop in each piece one at a time. They will be amazed at the fizzing. And, as I believe with everything, they can always add glitter if they want. Screw the cap on and shake it up!

Chapter 14: Rainbow Milk

This is another cool activity that will teach some basic scientific principles while being super colorful, fun, and entertaining.

You will need:

- A glass pie pan or a small dish for the soap

- A cup of milk

- Some liquid dish soap

- Q-tips

- Food coloring

Allow the child to pour the cup of milk into the pie pan and add a few drops of food coloring in the colors of their choice. Put the dish soap into the other, smaller dish, and allow them to dip the Q-tip into it. Tell them to put the Q-tip in the milk dish and watch the surface tension move the colors around in the pie pan. That's it!

Chapter 15: Fizzy Volcano

I firmly believe that everyone needs to make a fizzy volcano at least once in their lifetime, whether it's for a science fair or just for fun. Traditionally as kids, we all made our volcano bases from papier-mâché, which is another chapter in this book, but you can also make it out of play dough. Of course, the main ingredients for the chemical reactions here are baking soda and some kind of vinegar.

You will need:

- A pan (to avoid mess)

- A vase or other container, although the shape of a vase works especially well

- Play dough

- Baking soda

- Food coloring

- Vinegar

You're going to place the vase on the pan, and according to the skill of the person helping the child, or the skill and age of the child doing the project, you're going to use the vase and play dough to create the look of a volcano. Of course, you want to leave the top open. Have the child put the baking soda into the vase, add a combination of food coloring, and when you're ready, add the vinegar for the "eruption." This is experiment is always fun, even for the kids that are supervising the younger ones.

Chapter 16: Crayon Etching Art

Aside from the fizzy volcano, this was my other favorite activity as a child. It makes drawing that much more fun because there's an extra step and paint involved, plus, I still enjoy the revealing aspect of it.

You will need:

- White or neutral colored paper—You can use thicker style coloring paper or plain computer paper

- Crayons

- Black tempera paint

- Toothpicks

As with the crayon transfer project, have the child color or draw whatever they want onto the paper, but have them press down very hard to get as much wax onto the paper as they can. Paint the drawing with a thin layer of the black tempera paint and hang it up to dry completely. After it's dry, let the children draw onto the painted paper with the toothpicks, revealing the colors underneath in their drawings.

Chapter 17: Glittery Play Dough

If you have a child who plays with a lot of play dough, have you had instances where you run out? No fear. Did you know that you can make your own play dough with just a few common kitchen ingredients? It doesn't last as long but it works just fine.

All you need is:

- A mixing bowl

- 1 cup water

- 4 cups flour

- 4 tablespoons cooking oil (veggie, olive, or canola will work just fine)

- 1.5 cups salt (whatever kind you have)

- Any combination of food coloring your child wants

- Any color of glitter your child wants

- Airtight storage containers

Put the water in the mixing bowl and add as much food coloring as you would like. Add your dry ingredients, and begin to mix it together. Add the oil, which will begin to make your play dough squishy. If the play dough is too dry, you can add more later, but I would suggest starting with one tablespoon of the oil and working your way up to the desired consistency. Then add the glitter. This is a recipe your child can do almost entirely by themselves, with your supervision. Once the glitter is added, knead until it's good to go. Then you can let your child play with it, and when they're finished, store it an airtight storage container until next time. If it starts to get a little funky or dry, just chuck it and make a new batch.

Chapter 18: Duct Tape Magnets

All kids love magnets, and what's better than one they've made themselves? This is so simple, and you can make the magnets whatever designs they want.

You will need:

- Duct tape in various colors
- Scissors
- Small magnets
- Cardboard
- Pens/markers/paint pens

Cut out a square of cardboard and place onto a wide strip of tape. Place the magnet on the back of the cardboard square and fold the tape neatly over it. Add more layers of duct tape until it's fully wrapped and to the thickness you want. Trim any excess. Write or draw whatever letter or shape you want on the front, and paint or color it in using the markers. Sharpies work well. Then stick them to the fridge to hold up other art projects, like the crayon etching!

Chapter 19: Monster Claws

These are great for winter or for Halloween if your child wants to be a monster, and it's oh so simple.

All you need is:

- Felt
- Scissors
- Hot glue
- Gloves

Let your child pick out what color felt and gloves they would like before beginning. Measure the width of each glove finger and draw out some claws on the felt. The easiest route is for them to be triangle, but they could also be more curved if your child wants. Cut them out, and tuck each glove's fingertip slightly back into the glove. Glue the claw onto the tucked-in fingertip, so that when your child puts their hands in the gloves, the claw is in the correct position. You could even allow your child to assist in the gluing process, if you allow the glue to cool just slightly before handing them the claw. Be sure to wipe off any excess glue so it doesn't dry funky. Once they're fully dry, your child can wear them all the time.

Chapter 20: Snow Globes

This project is really similar to the above glitter jar, except I like it better because, like a traditional snow globe, you can help your child pick out small plastic toys (like the ones that come in the tubes at Michael's) to create a miniature scene.

You will need:

- A Mason jar (or a larger decorative jar for a larger scene) with a lid

- Water

- Glycerin

- A hot glue gun (and glue, obviously)

- Plastic toys of choice

- Glitter/sequins

- A spoon

Glue your toys down to the jar lid and let them dry completely. Fill the jar with water, leaving enough room for glitter, sequins, glycerin, or smaller plastic toys that can float around in there. Add in all the above extra components. Screw the top on and flip upside down so that it's going the right way. If you're nervous about the jar leaking, you could also seal it up with some extra glue and let it dry.

Chapter 21: Paper Bouquets

There are so many different ways to make a paper bouquet, and both are much more inexpensive than buying flowers, real or fake. Plus, children love to make things. I remember once, when I was about twelve, I recommended doing this for a party my mom had. It may require some adult supervision with younger kids, but it'll still be super fun.

You will need: (it will vary with however many flowers you are planning on making, so just eyeball it)

- 12 large sheets of tissue paper

- 12 pipe cleaners in complementing colors

- Scissors

- A vase

- Ribbon

- A ruler

Lay three different colored sheets of tissue paper, unfolded, on top of each other. It doesn't have to be the color of real flowers, just make sure they look good together. Make a one inch width fold, and then flip the paper and fold it back the opposite direction. If it's being done correctly, it should look like a paper fan by the time you are done.

Then, fold that in half and wrap the pipe cleaner around the bottom of it. Do this on alternating sides of the fan fold to create different flowers. You should be able to get about three flowers out of each fan folded paper. Doing it on either side creates differently colored flowers. Then cut the fan folded paper into the three flowers, and round off the edges. This step may require some help from an adult. After this is done, have your child hold the flower upside down by the pipe cleaner stem and pull gently down on the folds to reveal the petals. This can be a great exercise in gentleness. Pull all the layers out, and then flatten the middle out. Keep going until you've created a bouquet, and arrange them with a ribbon in the vase.

Chapter 22: Papier Mâché

This is an awesome project that I've always enjoyed, even up till now. It's so simple for kids to do, but it's also easy for them to refine into a real artistic skill as adults.

You will need:

- Newspaper

- Tempera or acrylic paint

- For the paste you can use white glue and water, water and flour, or a liquid starch. All can be found at the grocery store, you just need to figure out which option works the best for you. I have always preferred the water and flour method. If you heat the water a little bit, it will help the flour to stick better. Add salt to your paste for your project to last longer.

Pick out an item that you want to papier-mâché, and make sure it's cleaned and ready to go. Or, if you have a little artist on your hands, you can have them create a form from wire or wood. Dip the newspaper in the mixture and do one layer, making sure to overlap as you go around your object. I find that it's best to allow the layers to dry just a little bit between them. Keep doing layers until you are satisfied with the shape of your object, but try to keep to the minimum so that you have less possibility for breakage, shapelessness, or molding. That's what the salt in the paste is for. This may take some restraint on the part of the kids.

Once your papier-mâché is dry, you'll want to have the kids paint it with a thin layer of white tempera to make it easier to paint creatively. Let that paint layer dry before adding more paint and completing the masterpiece!

Chapter 23: Countdown Paper Chains

It's like the 90s version of a countdown clock but much more fun, especially for small kids, because they get to use their hands. While I mainly make these at the beginning of December as a way to get stoked for Christmas, you could make them for any holiday or as a countdown to birthdays or vacations.

Just pick out the right color paper for the holiday, or any color paper your child wants. I find that drawing paper or cardstock works best, especially since it's also fun to hang these up as garlands.

Cut the paper into strips and have the children make circles from the strips, looping them together into chains. After each loop, tape the paper to itself. Make as many loops for as many days the countdown is for. At the end or beginning of each day, allow your child to rip off a loop. This can also help improve young kids' counting skills.

Chapter 24: Friendship Bracelets

While friendship bracelets can easily be made by older kids using string or cord and a pattern, for younger kids, this version will be a little bit easier.

You will need:

- Toilet paper rolls
- Thread
- Scissors
- Tempera paint
- A hole punch

Cut the toilet paper roll in half on the long side and then again in the opposite direction. You should measure it against the child's wrist at this point to make sure it will fit. Tie the thread around the back to make it secure to the child's wrist. If it's too loose, it might be a good idea to hole punch the top and bottom and tie a string through it. Allow the child to create a crisscross or any other pattern by wrapping the string back against the cuff or back through the holes. Finally, paint the cuff and allow it to dry before wearing.

Chapter 25: Tie Dye T-shirts

Although I have written about how to make tie dye for adults, for children I'd like to make it a bit easier for kids. You can buy a tie dye kit, and aside from that, all you need is rubber bands and cotton t-shirts. You'll also want some gallon Ziplock bags.

Mix up the dye with hot water and then allow the kids to create their own wrap patterns. Have them put on some gloves and then put on the dye. Be sure to tell them that they can make any color they want from just red, blue and yellow. Once they're done, place the t-shirts into the Ziplock bags and give it at least eight hours.

With fresh gloves on, allow the kids to remove their shirts from the bags and rinse them out. Once dry, they can wear them!

Chapter 26: Water Xylophone

I think this is a great alternative to allowing small children to make music on pots and pans.

All you need for this is:

- Some empty glass bottles

- Water

- Different colors of food coloring

- A stick or something for the child to tap and hit the bottles with

Allow the child to fill up the bottles with differing amounts of water. Then let them put a different color food coloring in each bottle. As they play, make sure you point out to them that the different amounts of water and different sizes of bottles make different noises.

Conclusion

I hope that with this guide, you have plenty of ideas for your children. This would be an awesome guide that's great for any camp counselor who is stuck for ideas, as there is something in here for any age. And that means that most of the projects can be supervised by older children aged ten and up. This would also be great for children with special needs or ADD children. Physical and mental engagement can be a great alternative to punishment.

Any time you're stuck for ideas, just refer to this book, and I'm sure you'll find something fun to do. Also, engaging with your child in these activities can always be a fun opportunity to bond.

Finally, I'd like to thank you for purchasing this book! If you enjoyed it or found it helpful, I'd greatly appreciate it if you'd take a moment to leave a review on Amazon. Thank you!